My Reality
Angela Spugnardi

Copyright © 2018 Angela Spugnardi

All rights reserved.

ISBN:198644449X
ISBN-13:978-1986444491

This one's for me.

A WORD FROM THE ARTIST

I have dealt with far too much anger and skepticism over the years as though I've chosen to let my mental illness overcome me.

I did not choose this.

It was done to me.

Every day is another struggle to forget. Another attempt to savor one single second of my day where I am living in the present rather than in fear of the past.

I am alone in my suffering.

And I, alone, can defeat it.

Angela Spugnardi

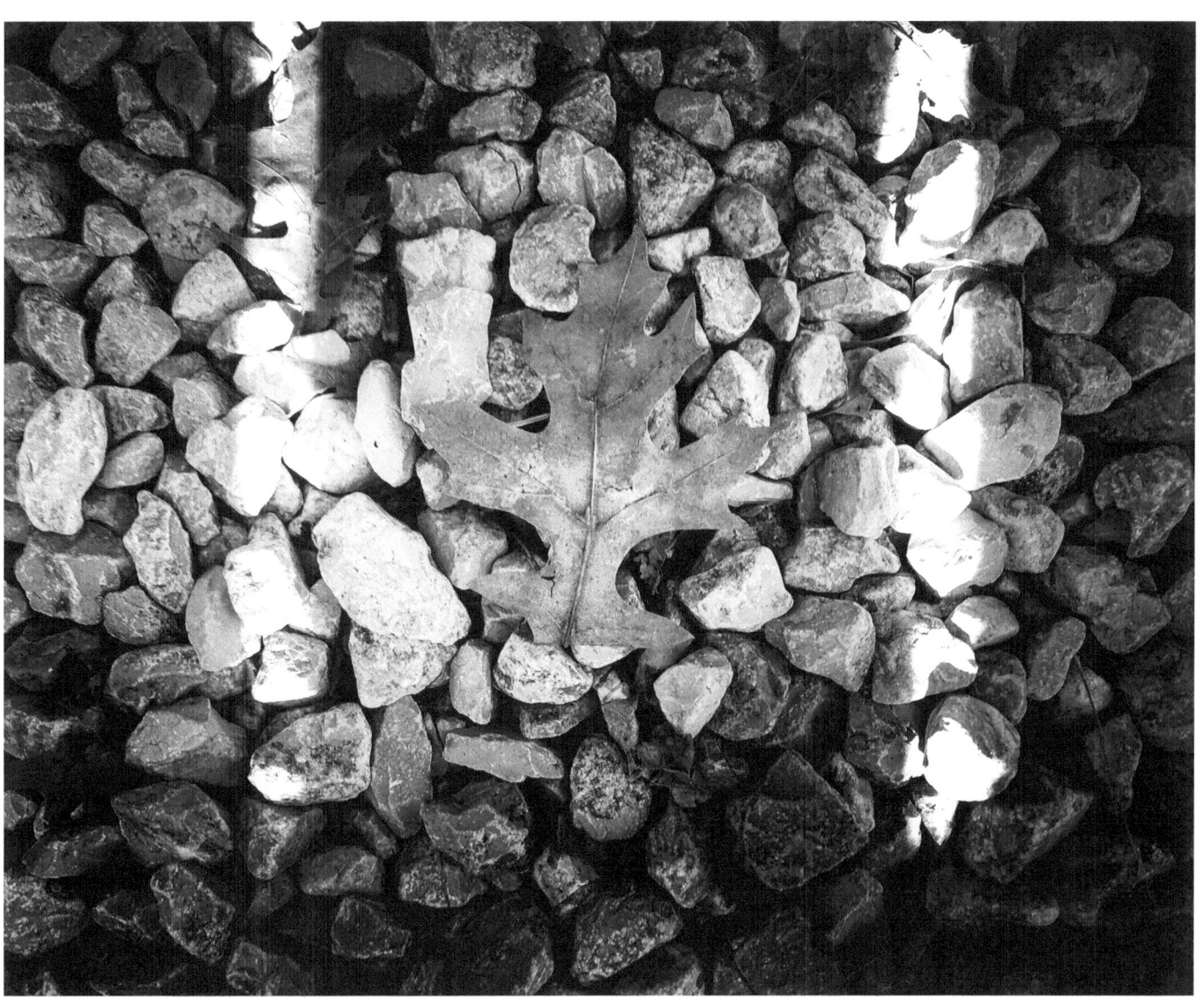

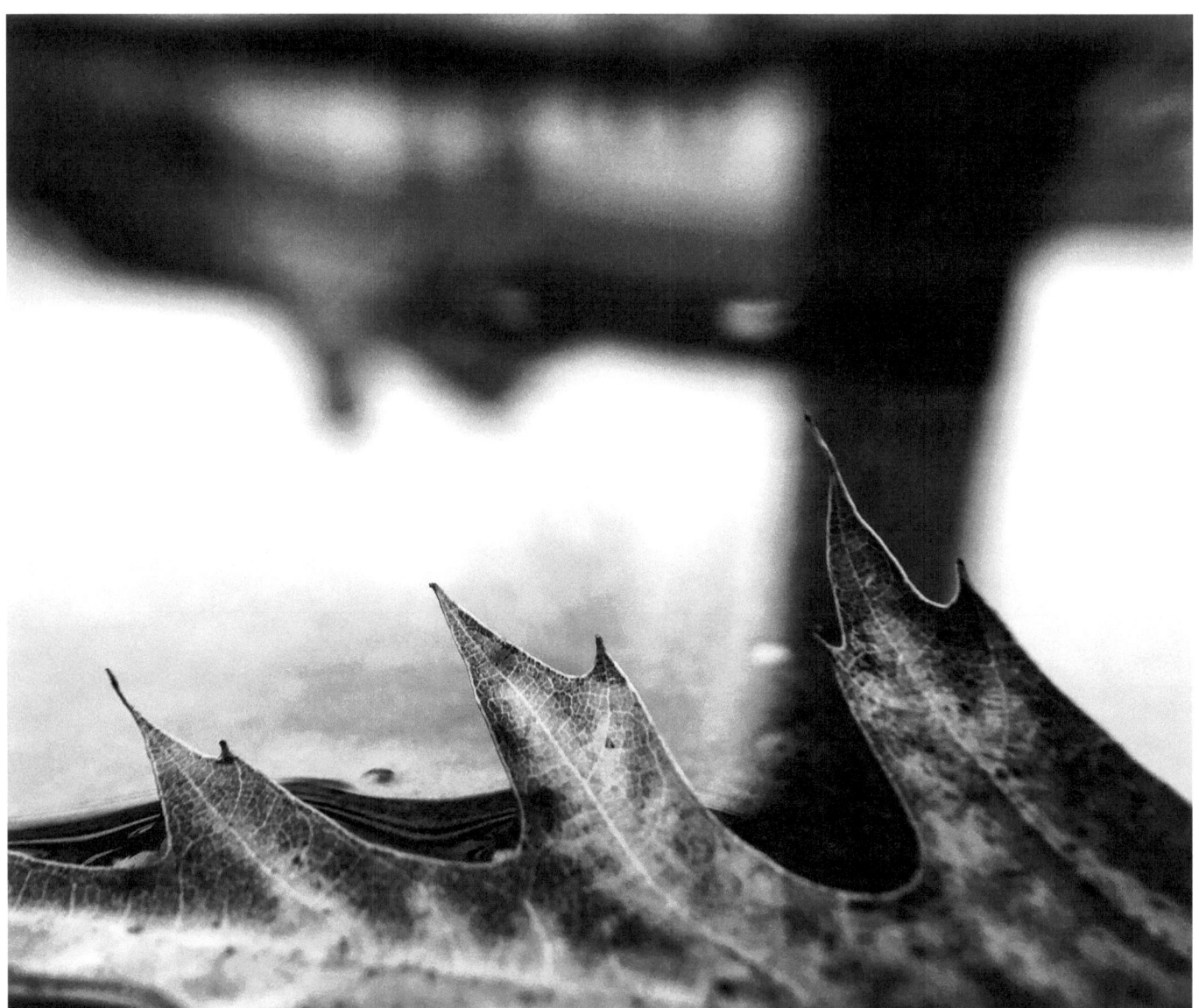

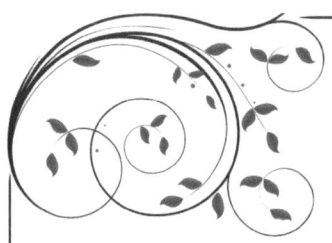

As my world falls to pieces, the shards of shattered dreams sink deeper into repression.

I hope they are lost.

I hope they are drowned in pools of tears.

I hope it was all a lie.

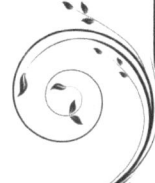

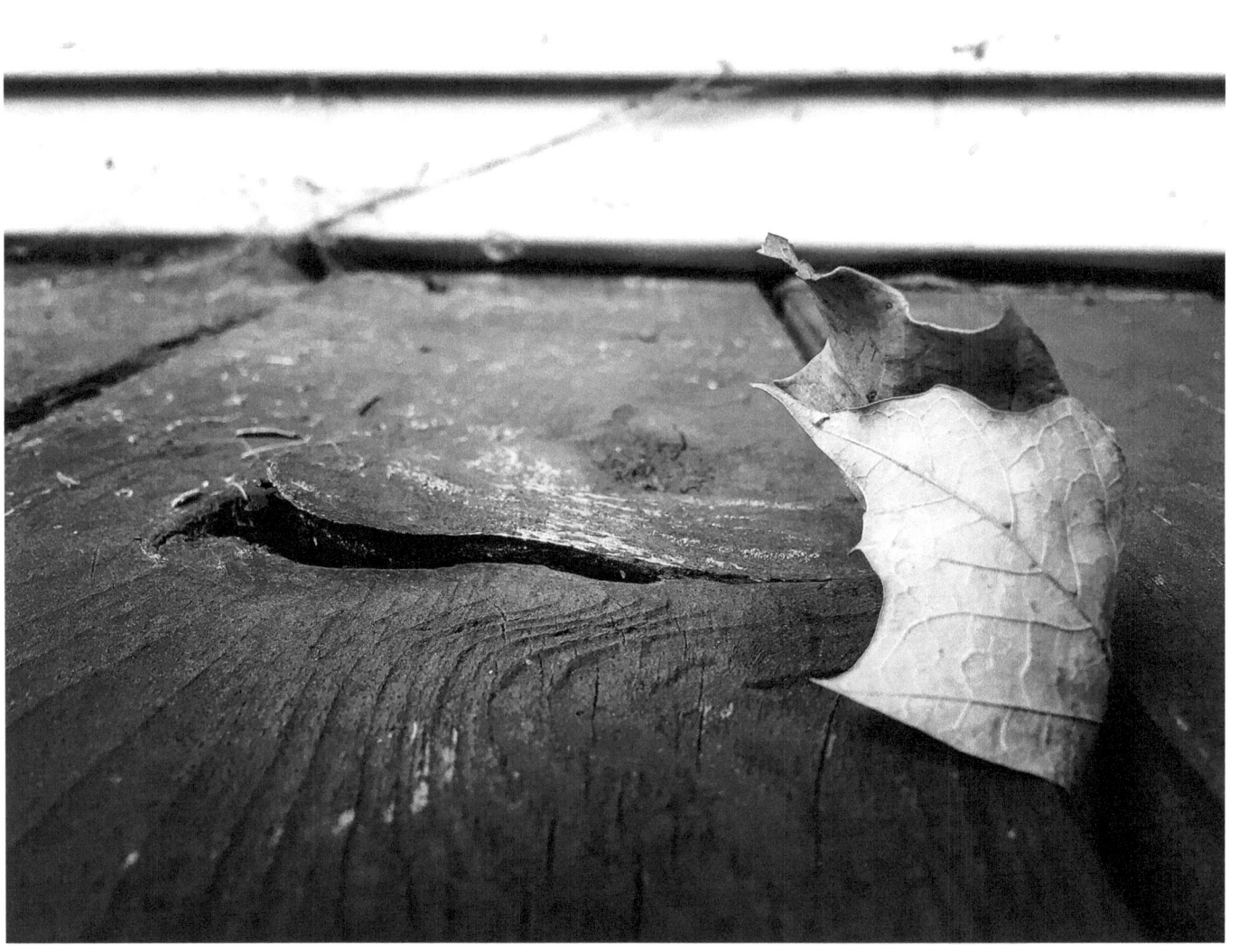

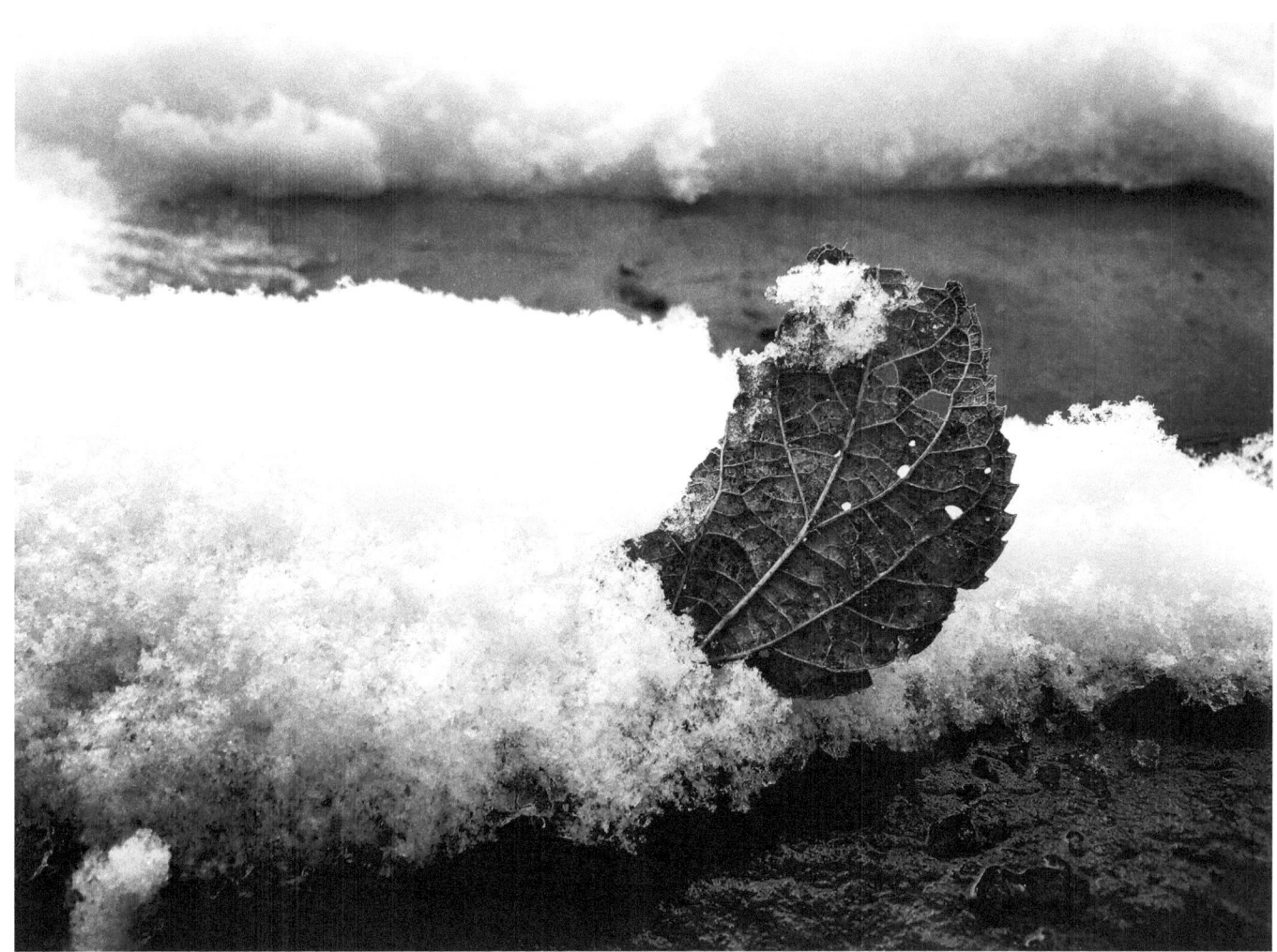

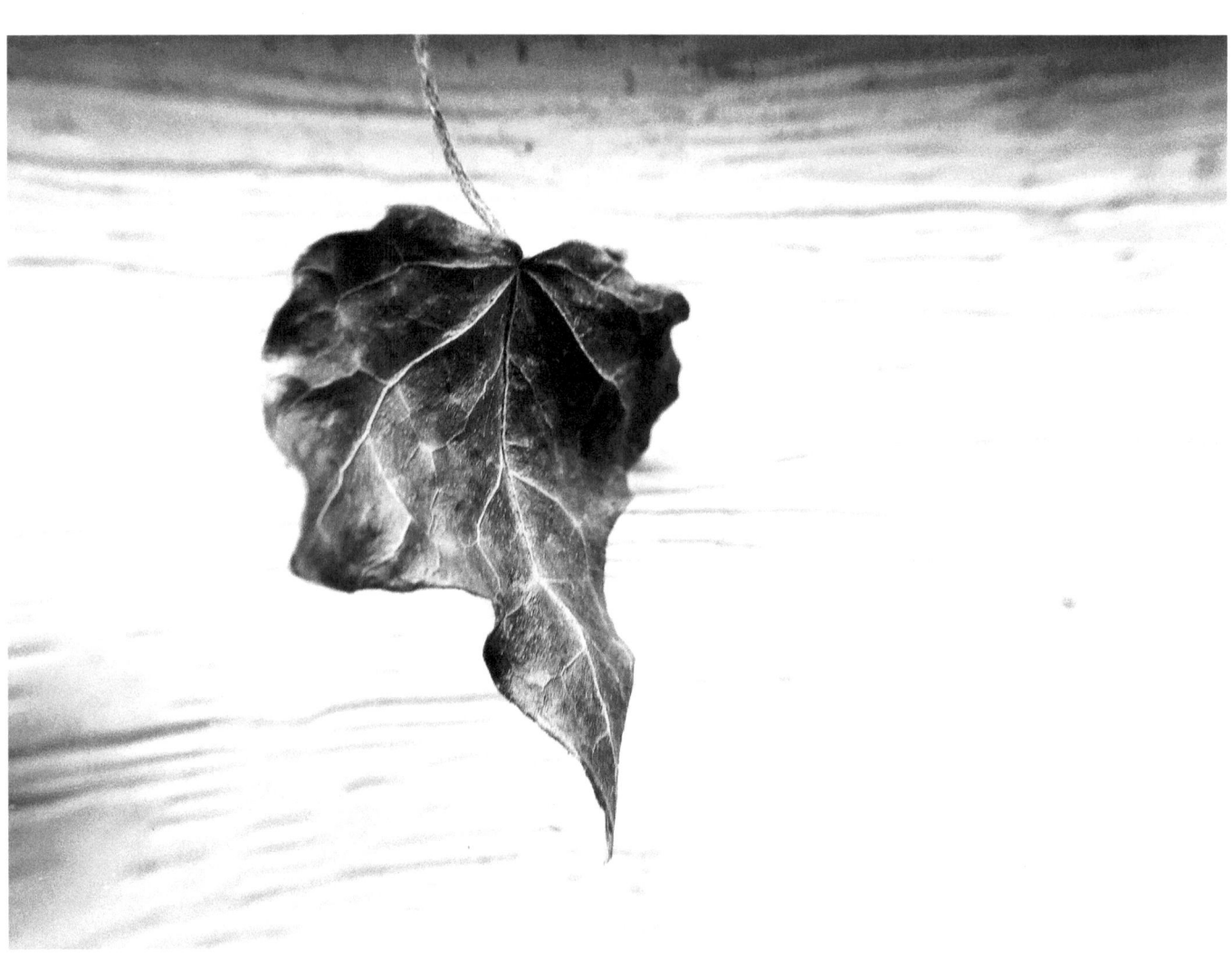

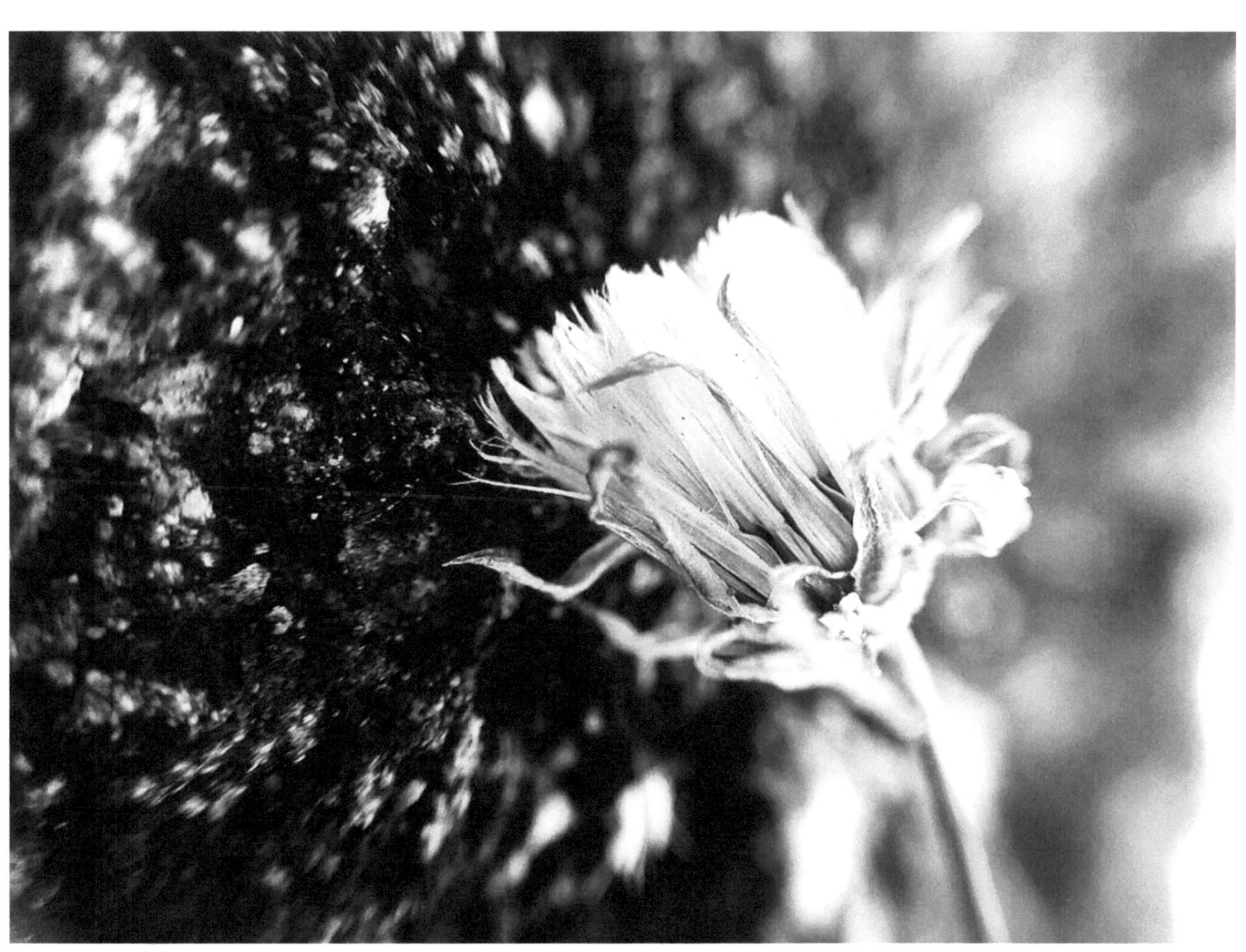

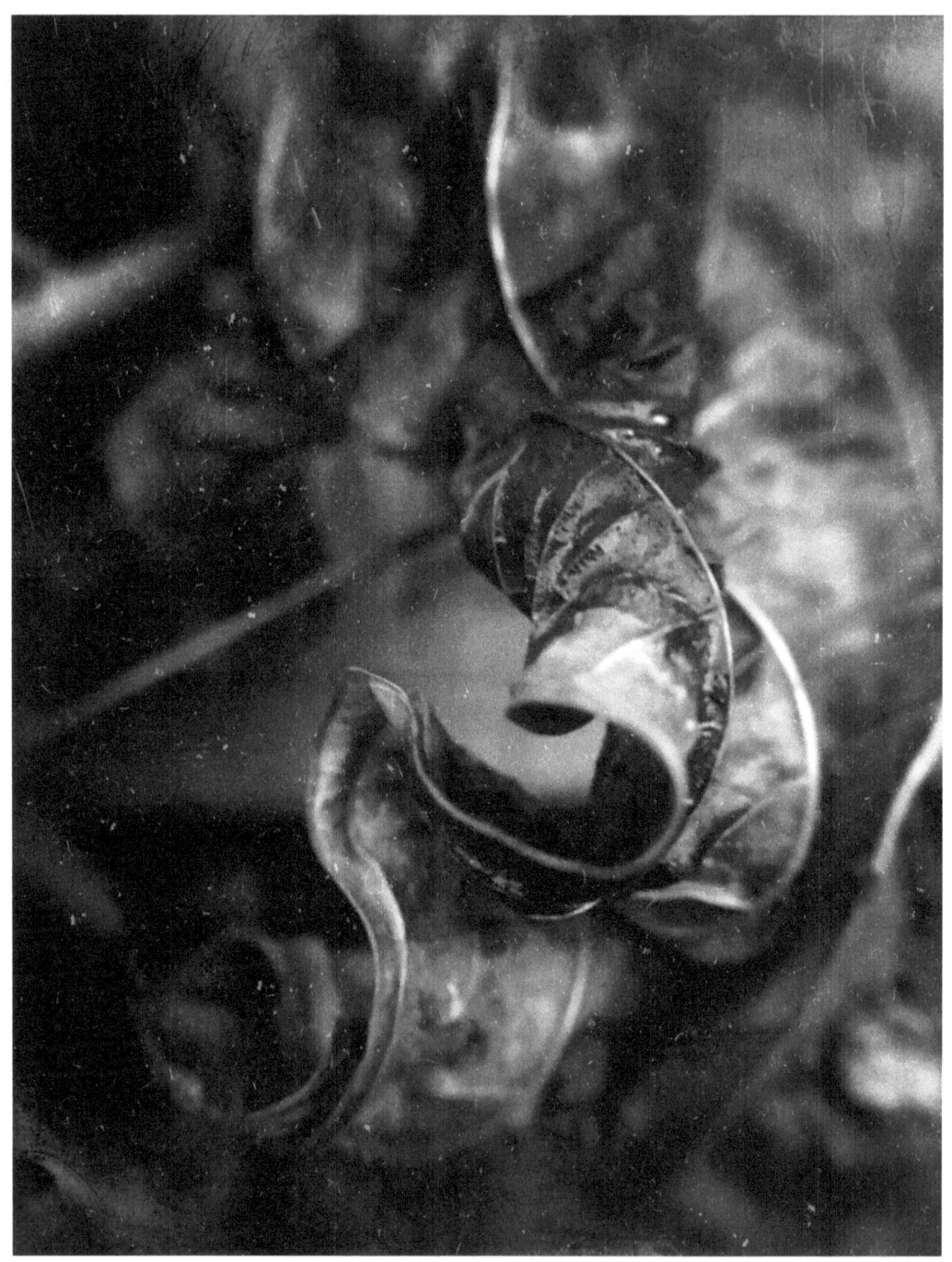

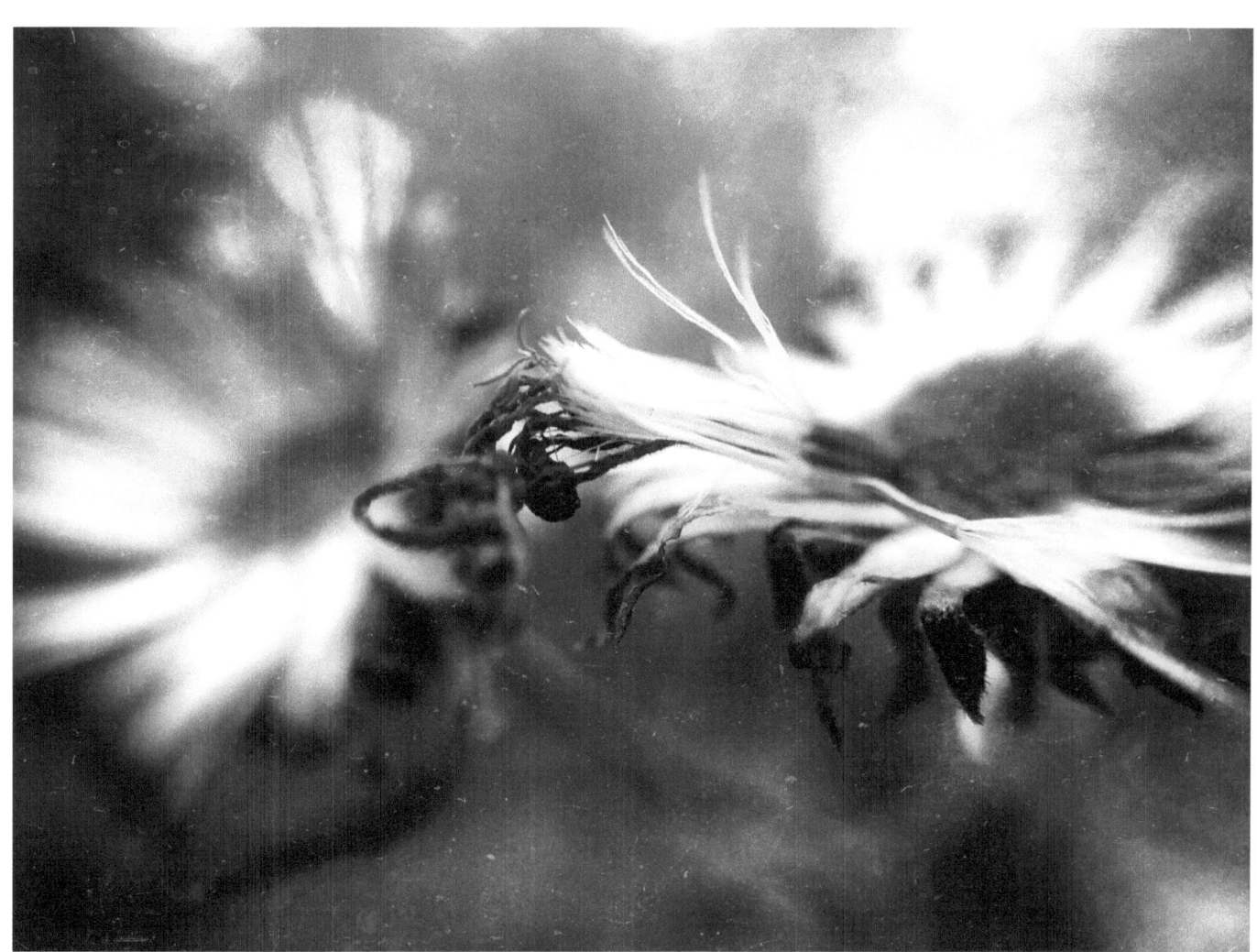

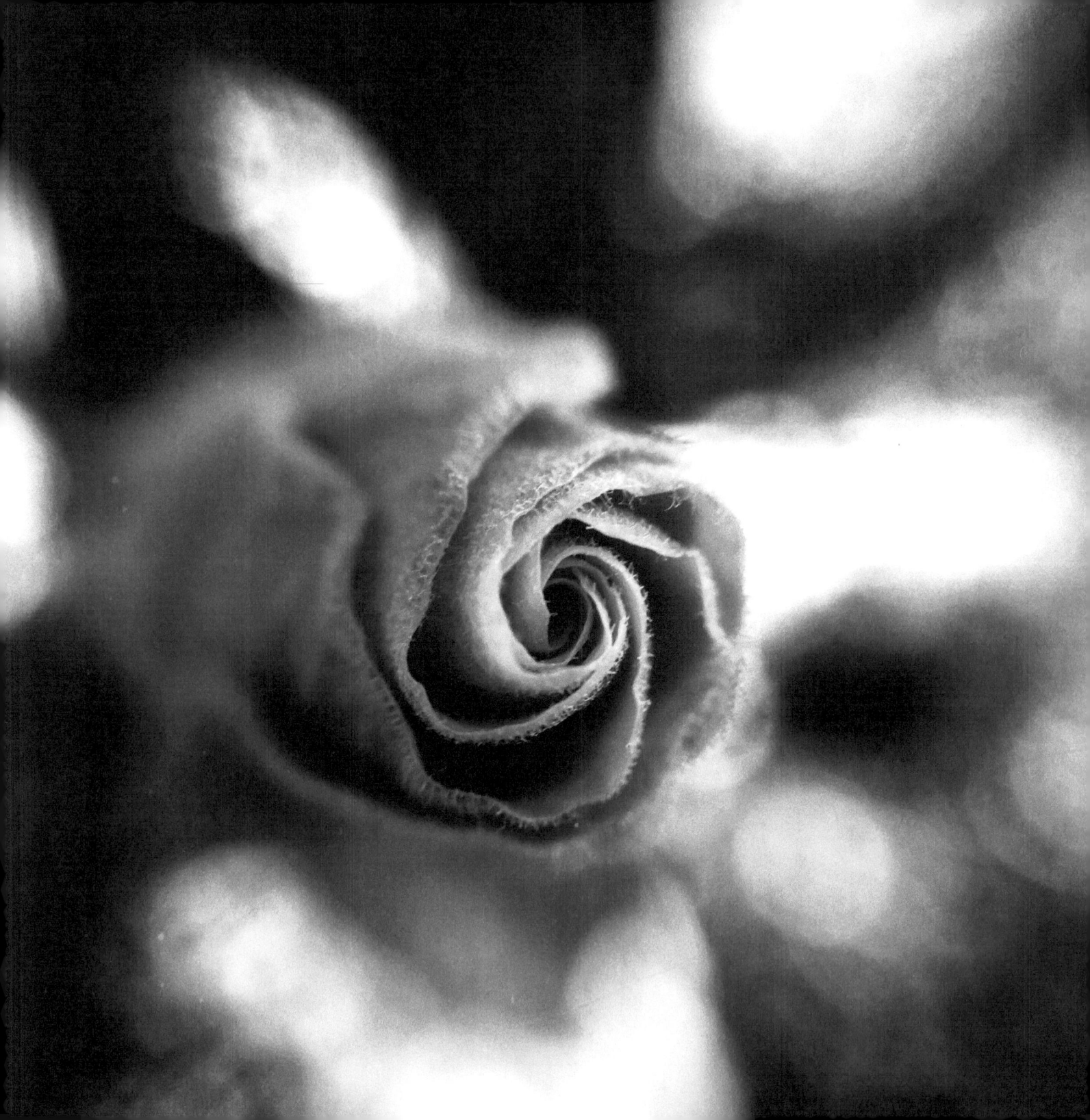

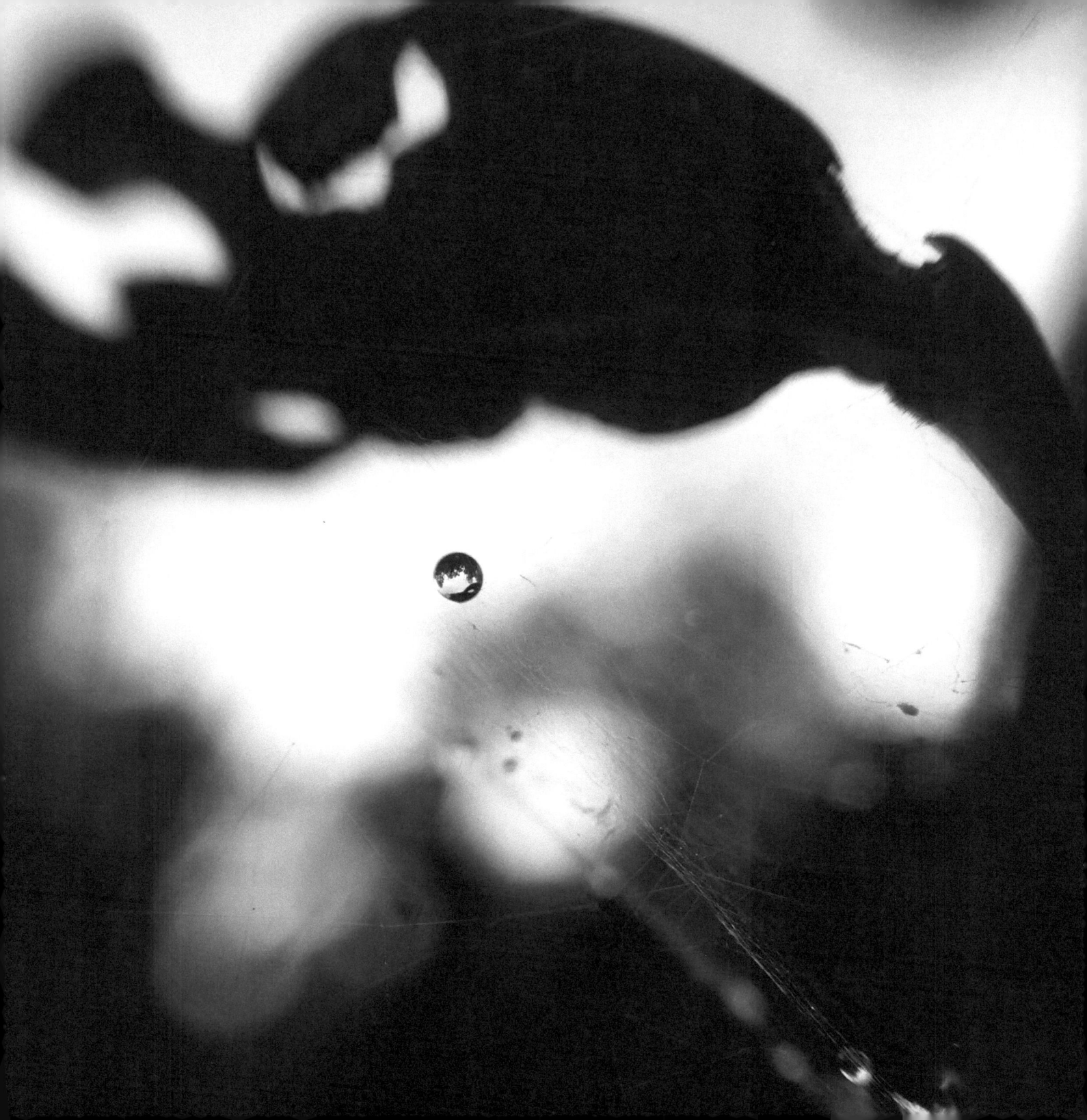

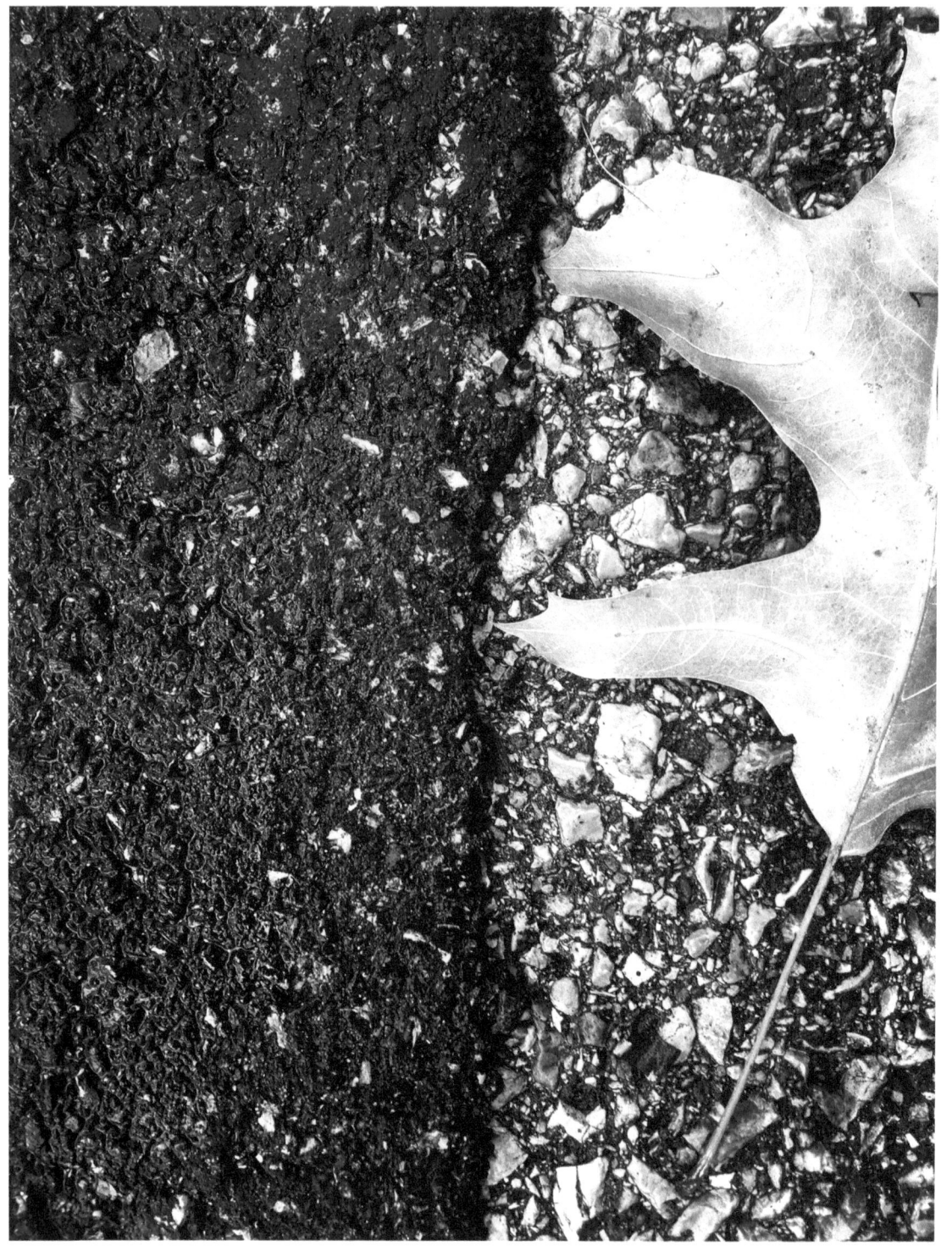

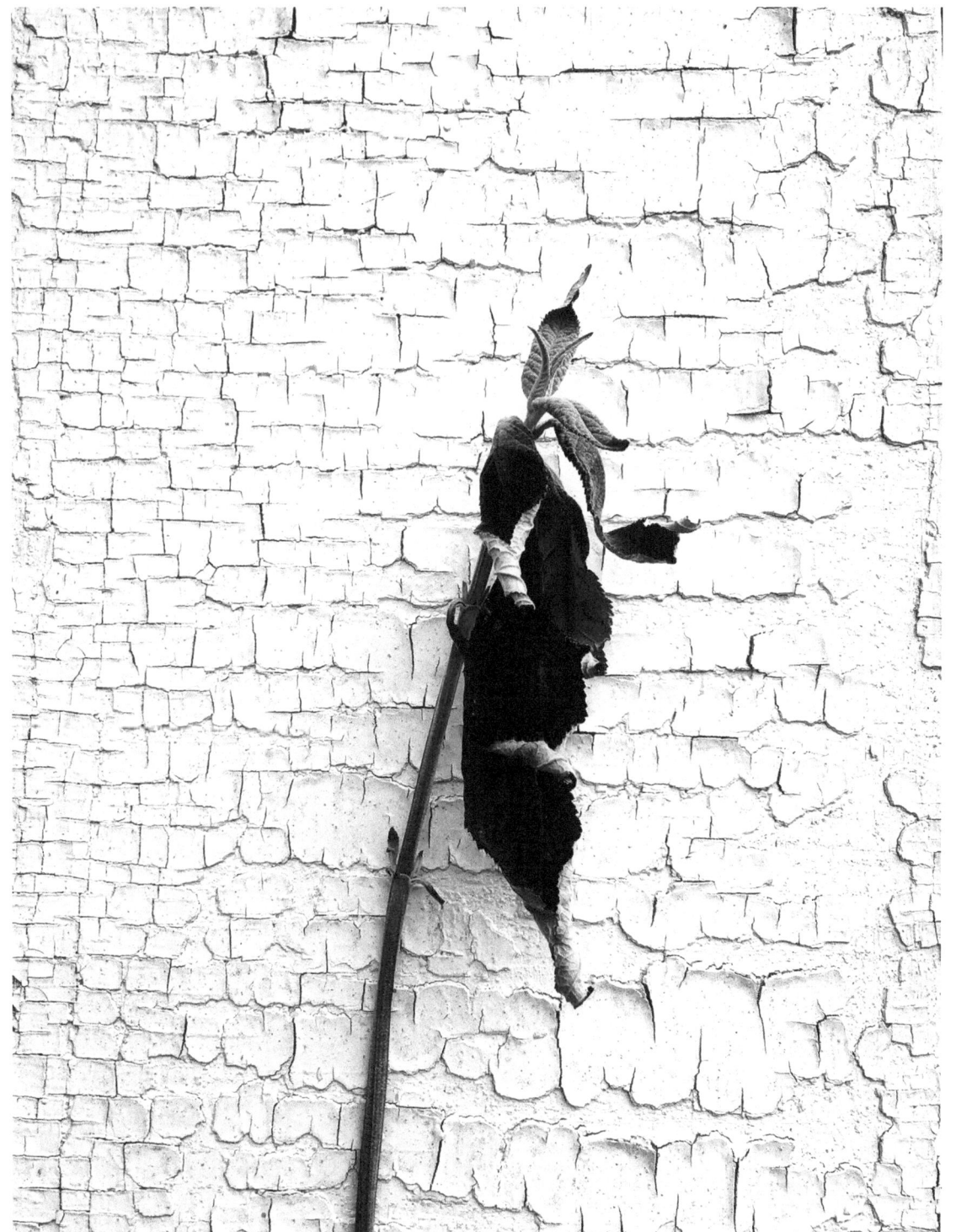

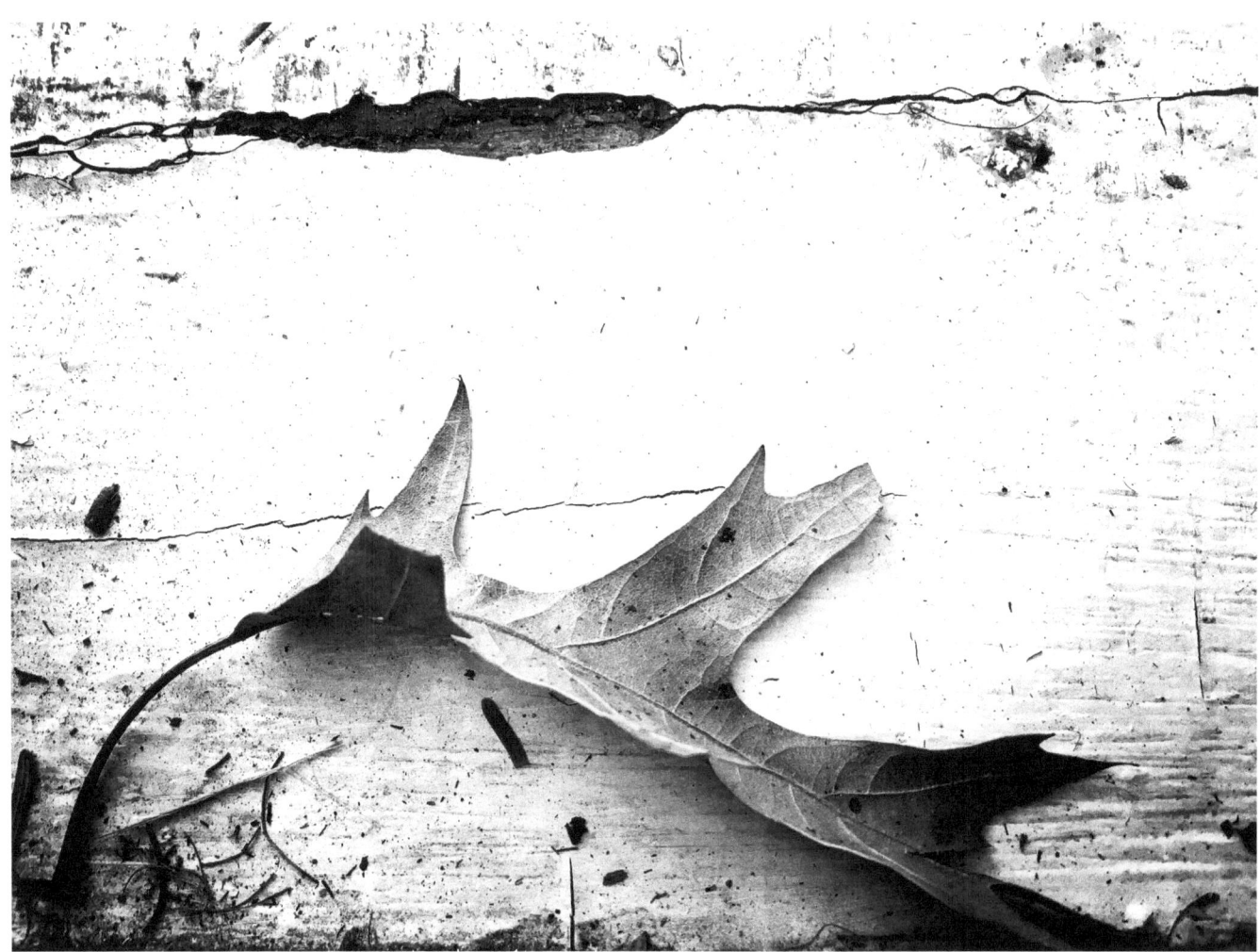

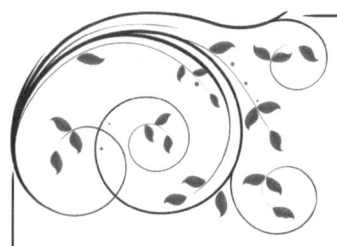

Like the fallen leaf, I feel disconnected from my life source.

There is no branch to cling to.

There is no breeze to carry me.

I am falling.

I am wilting.

And soon there will be nothing left of me.

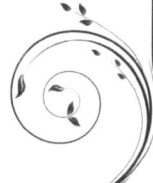

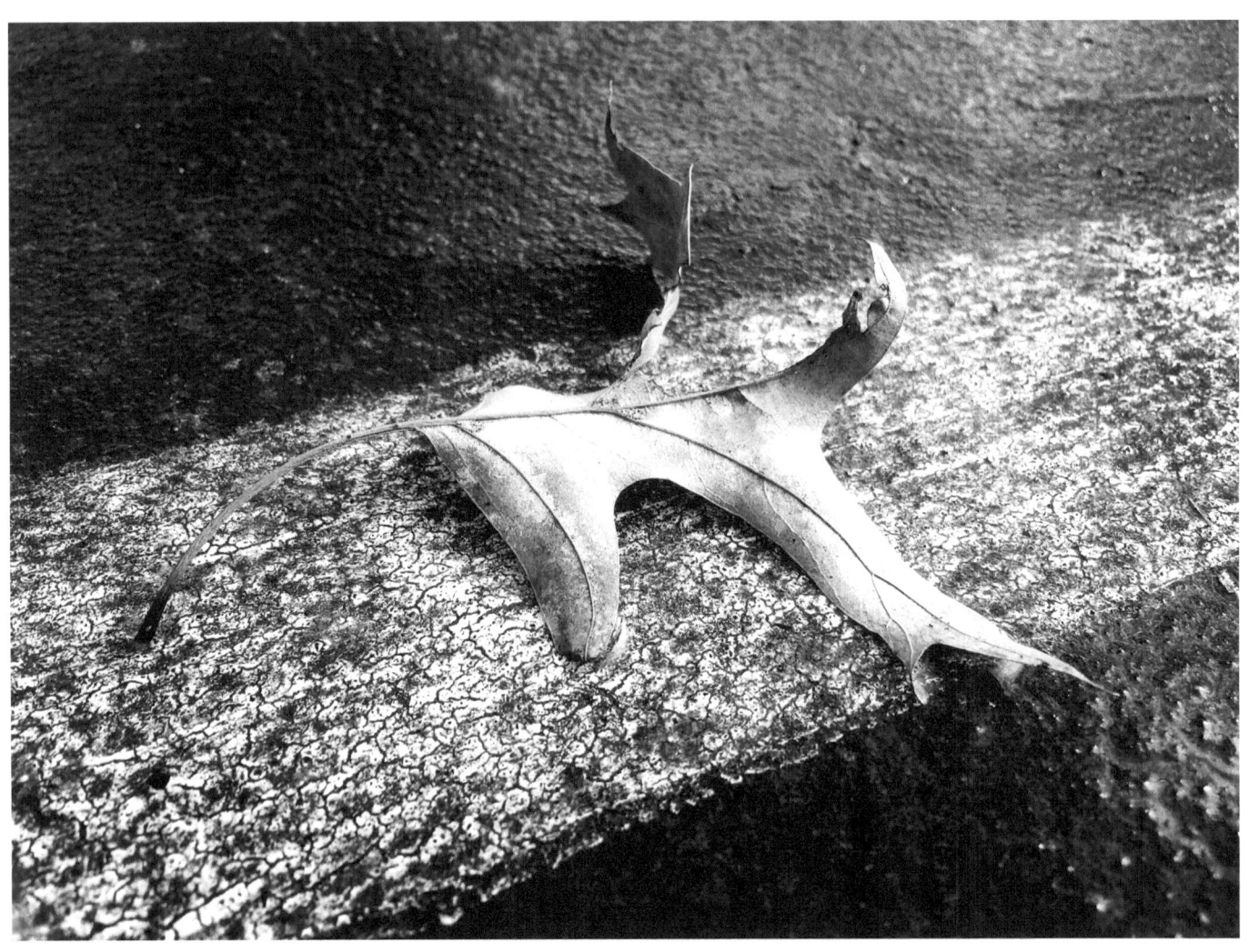

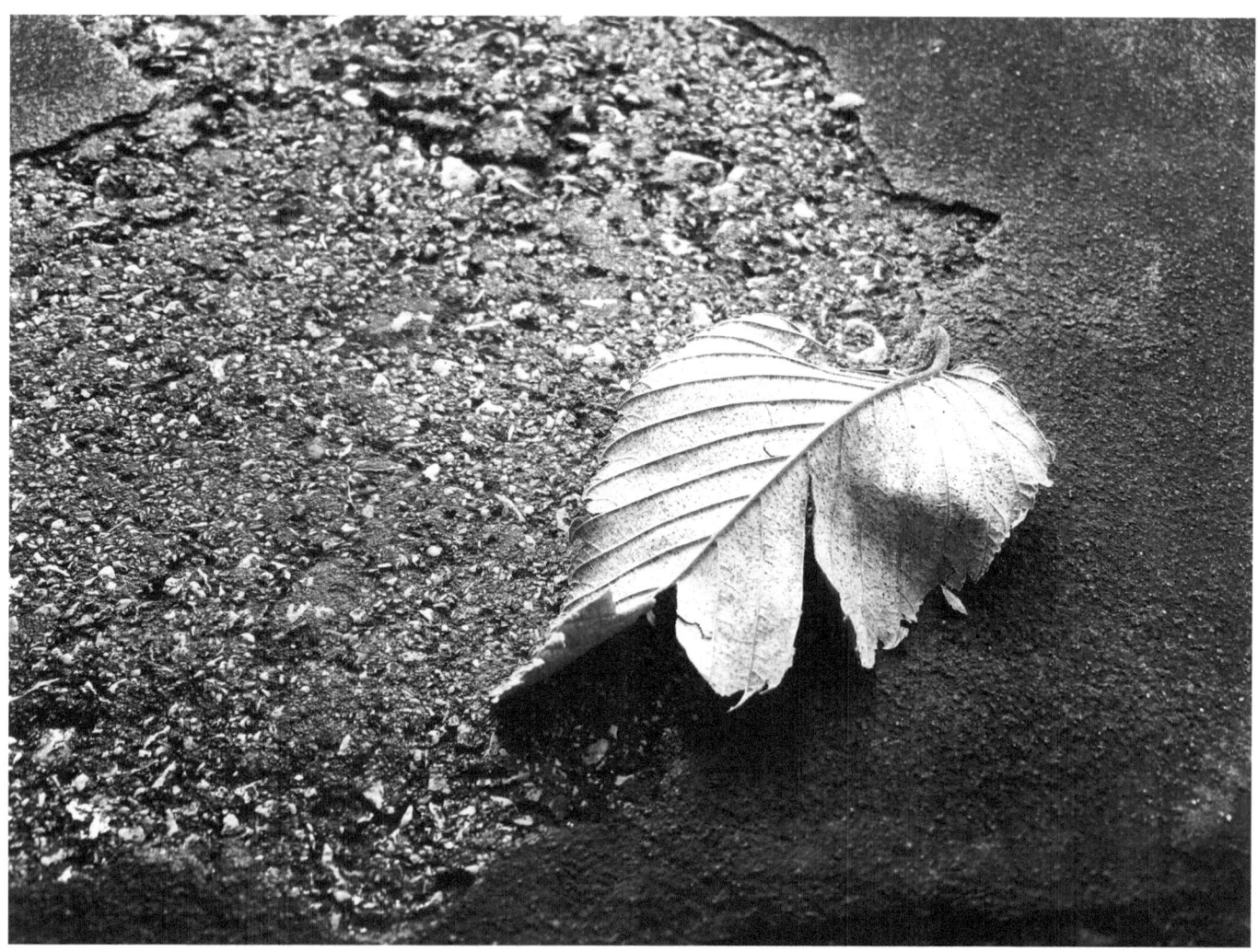

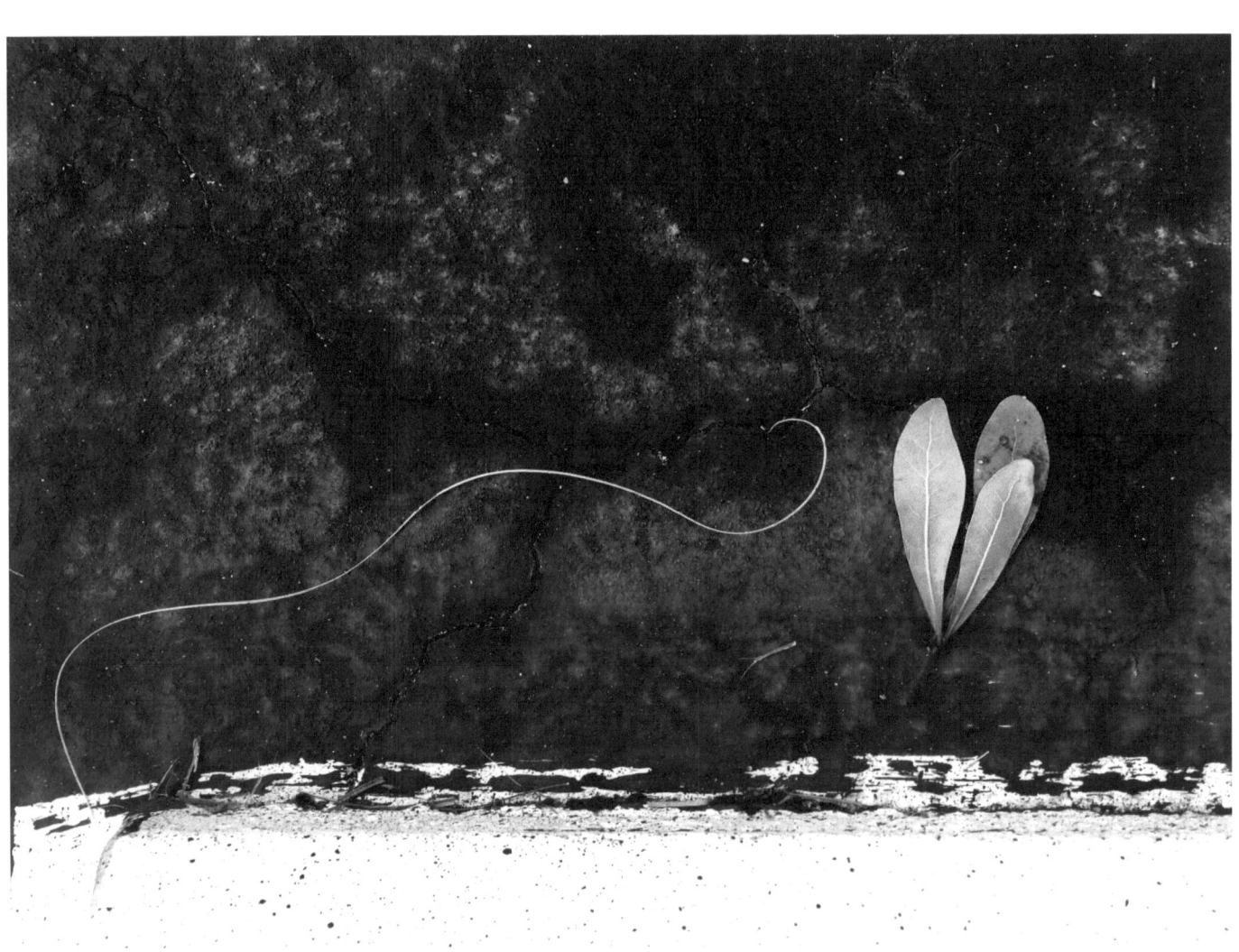

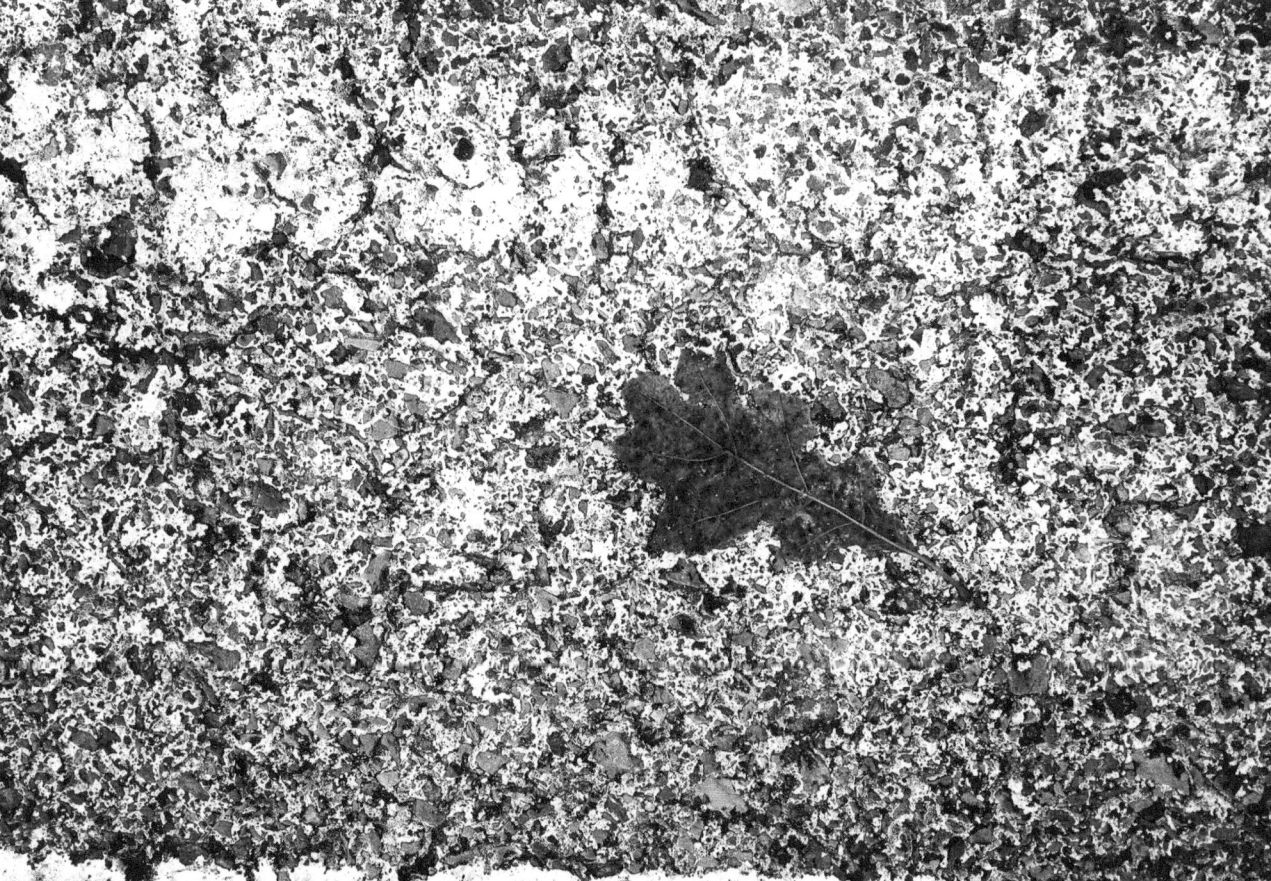

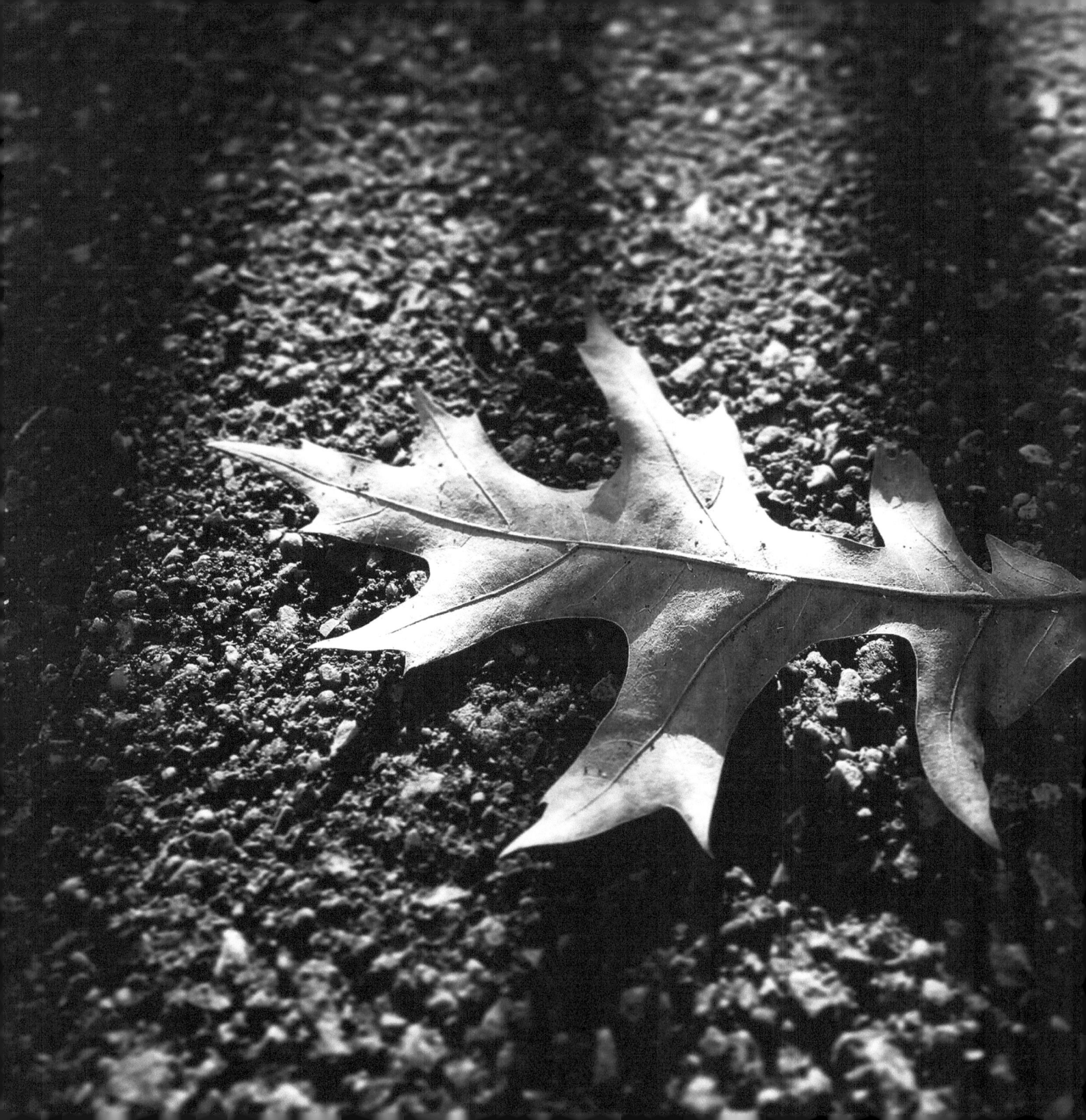

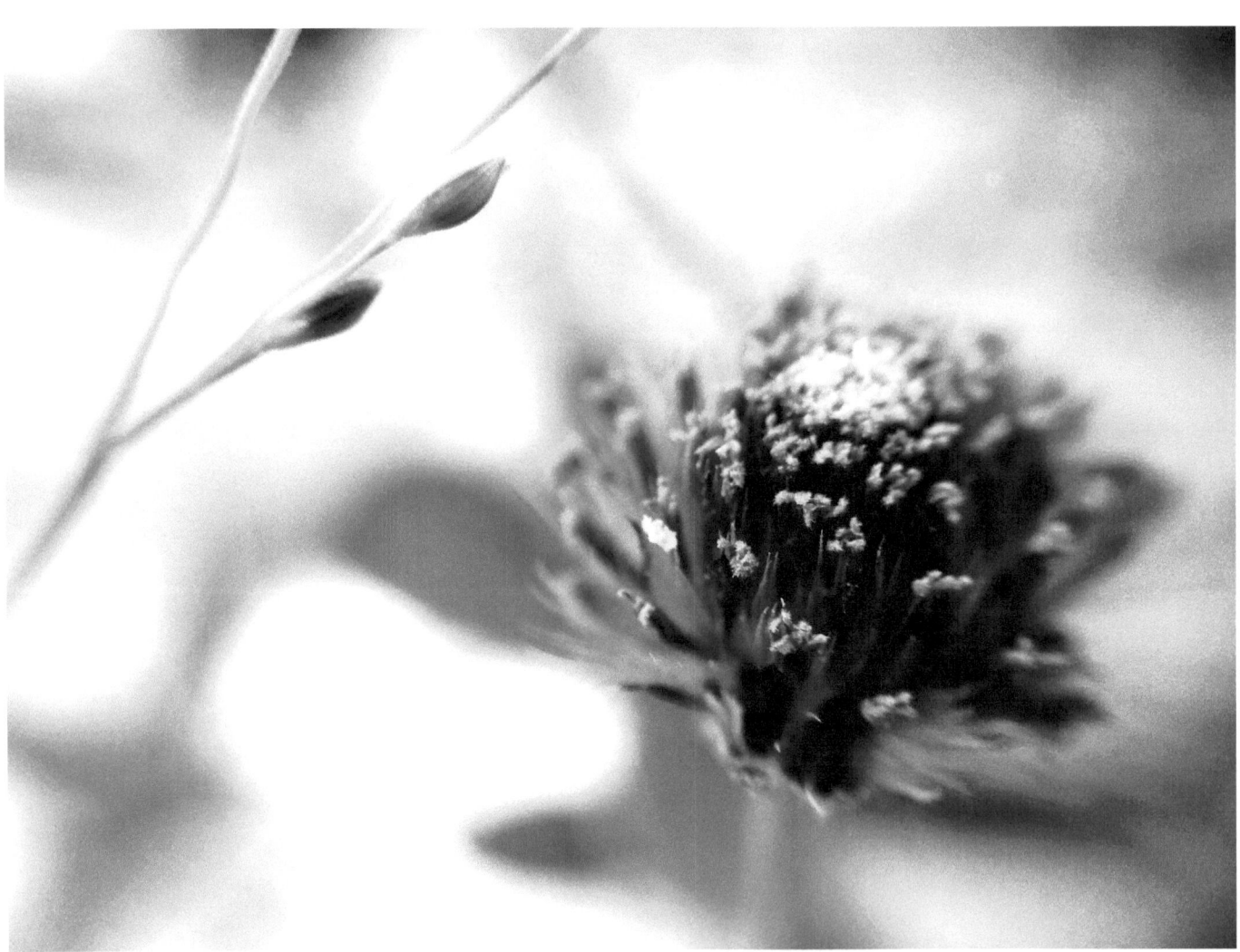

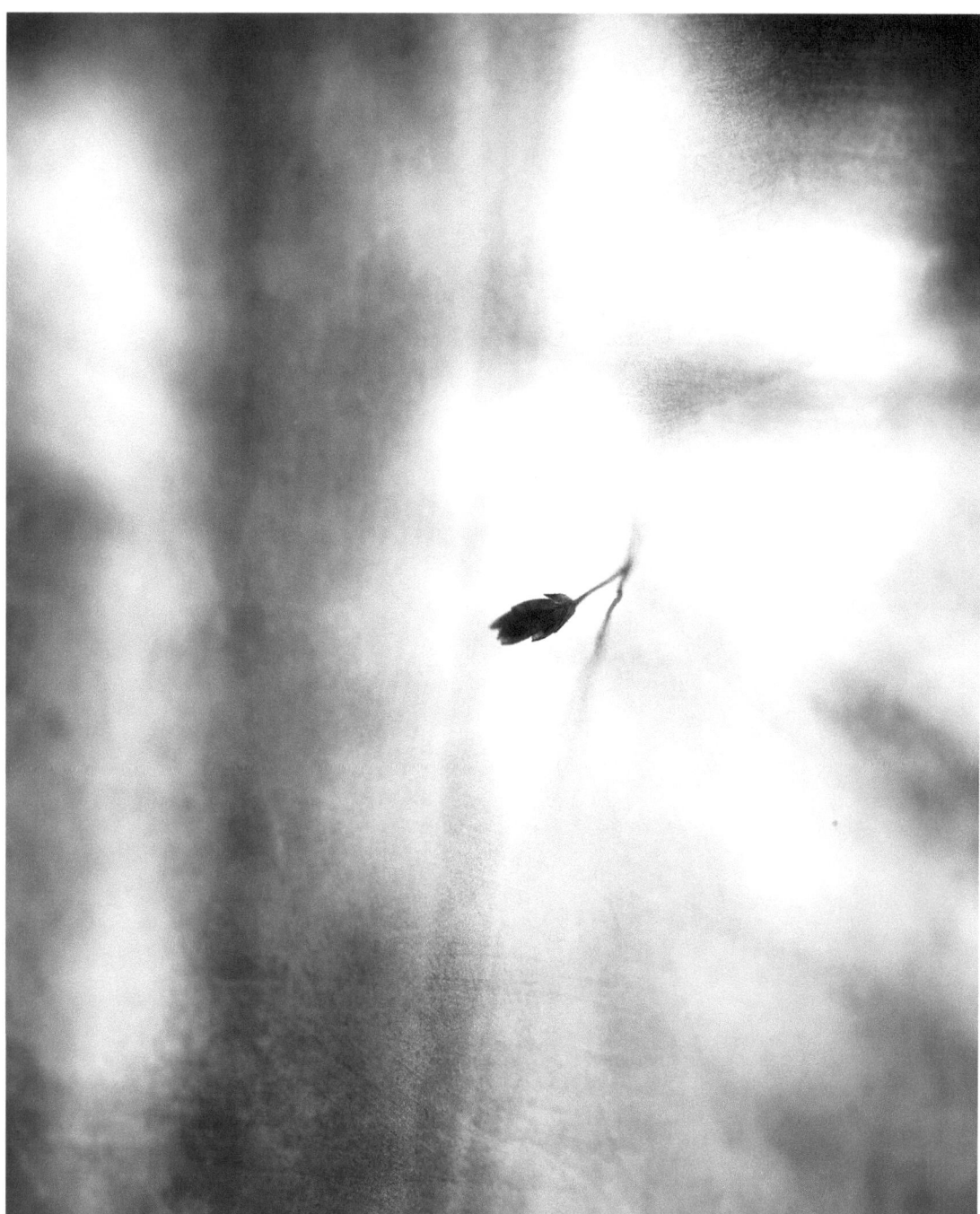

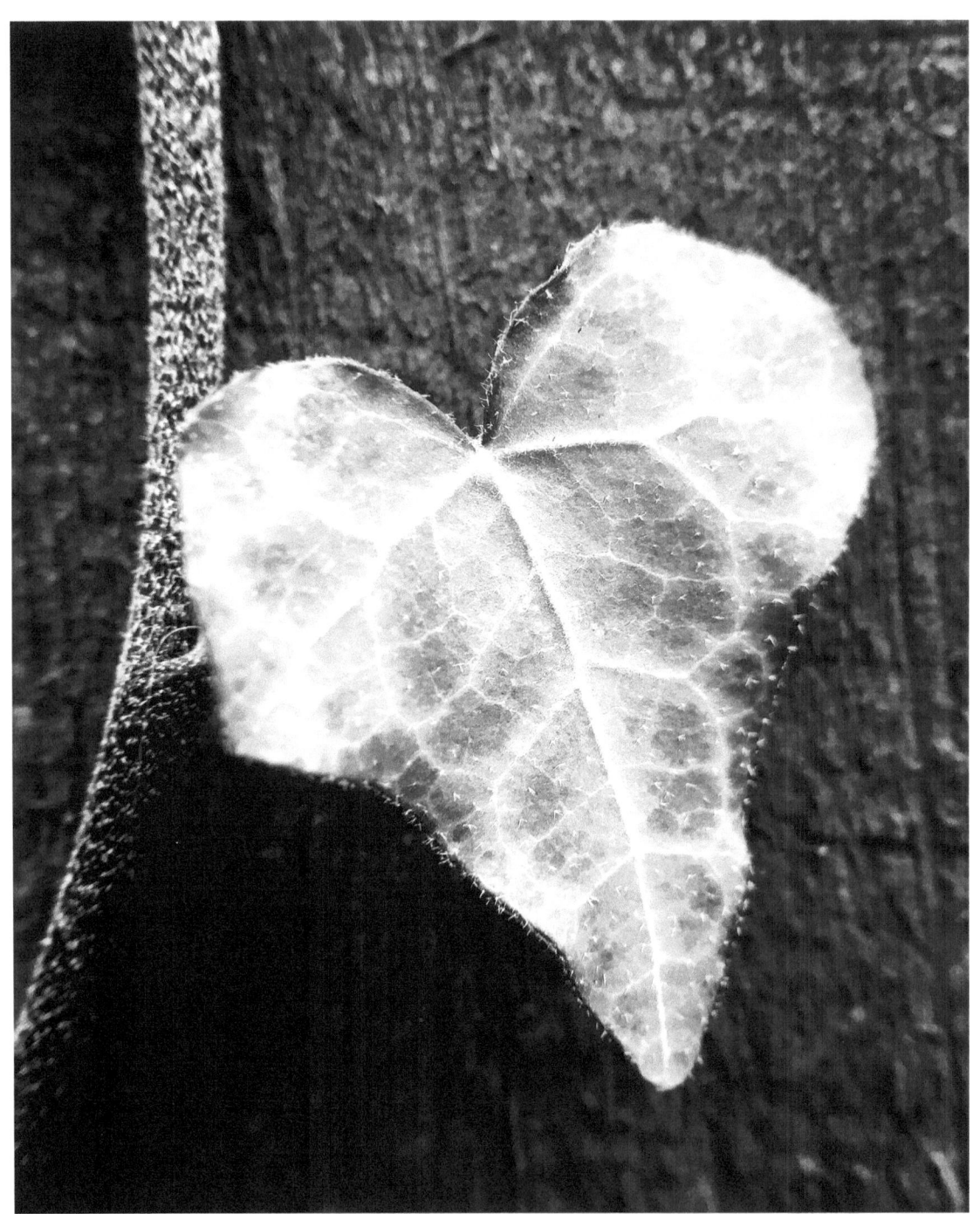

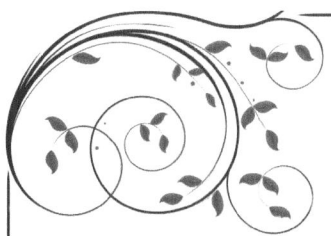

My heart once was beautiful.

Now it is simply broken.

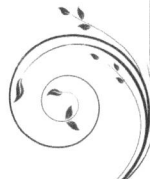

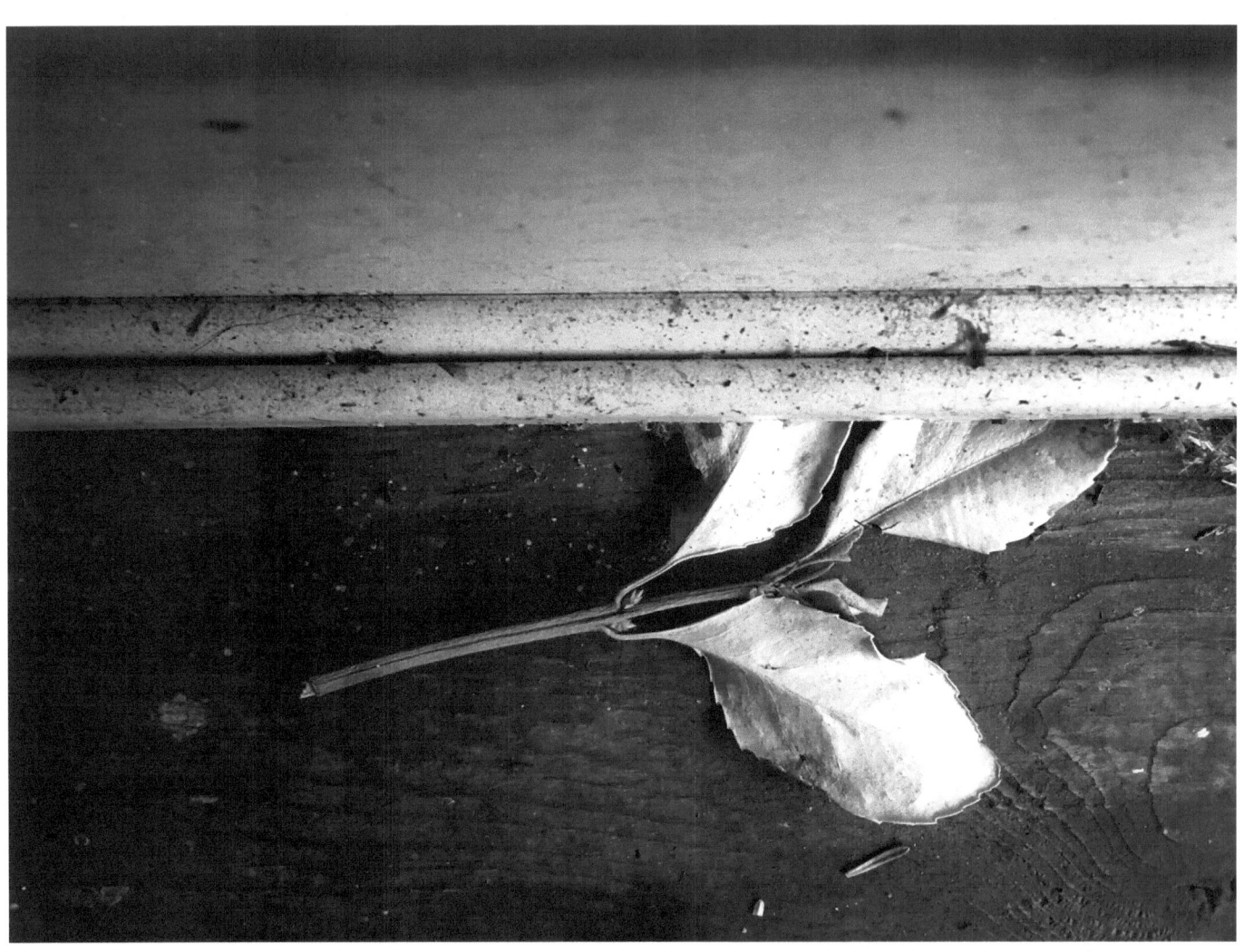

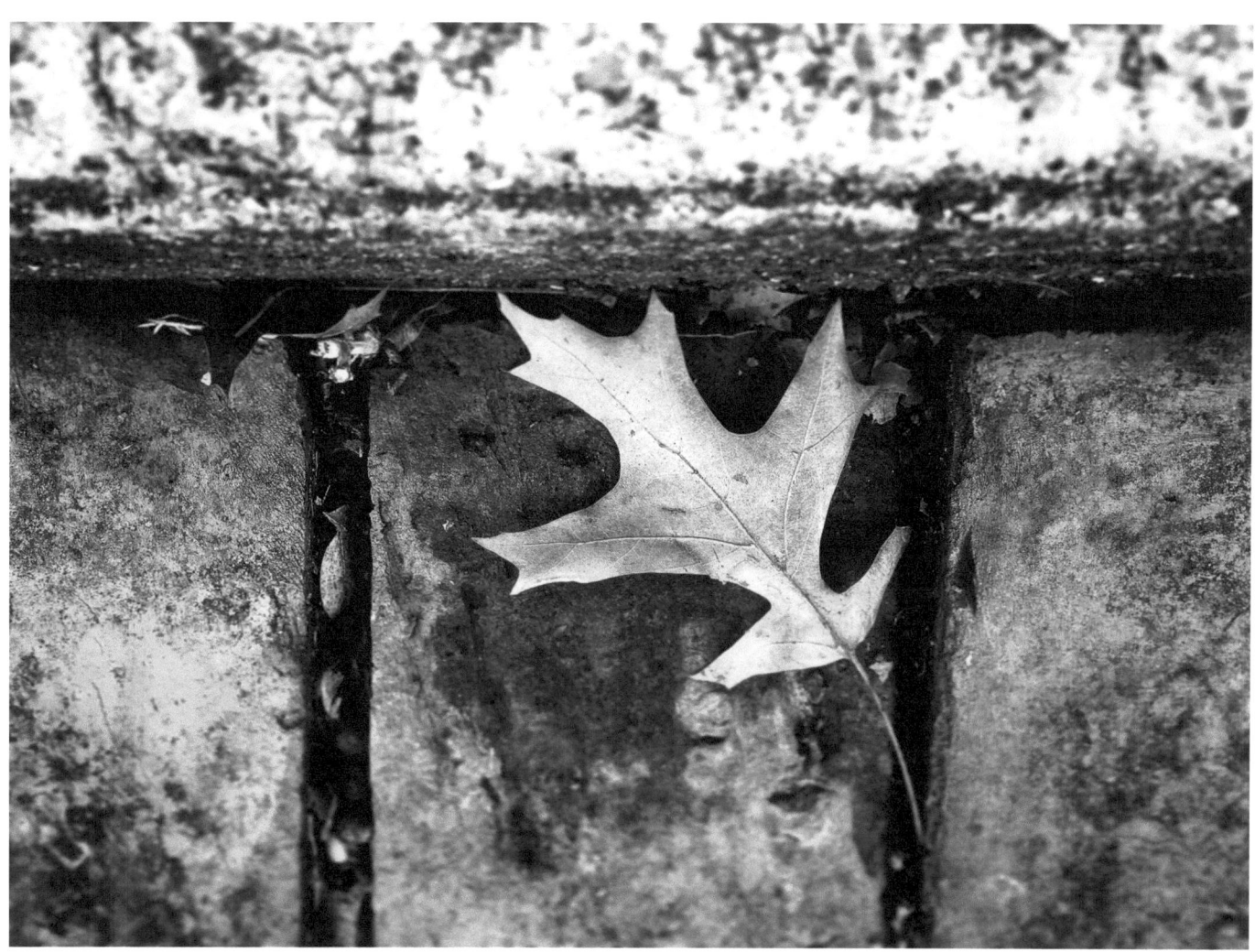

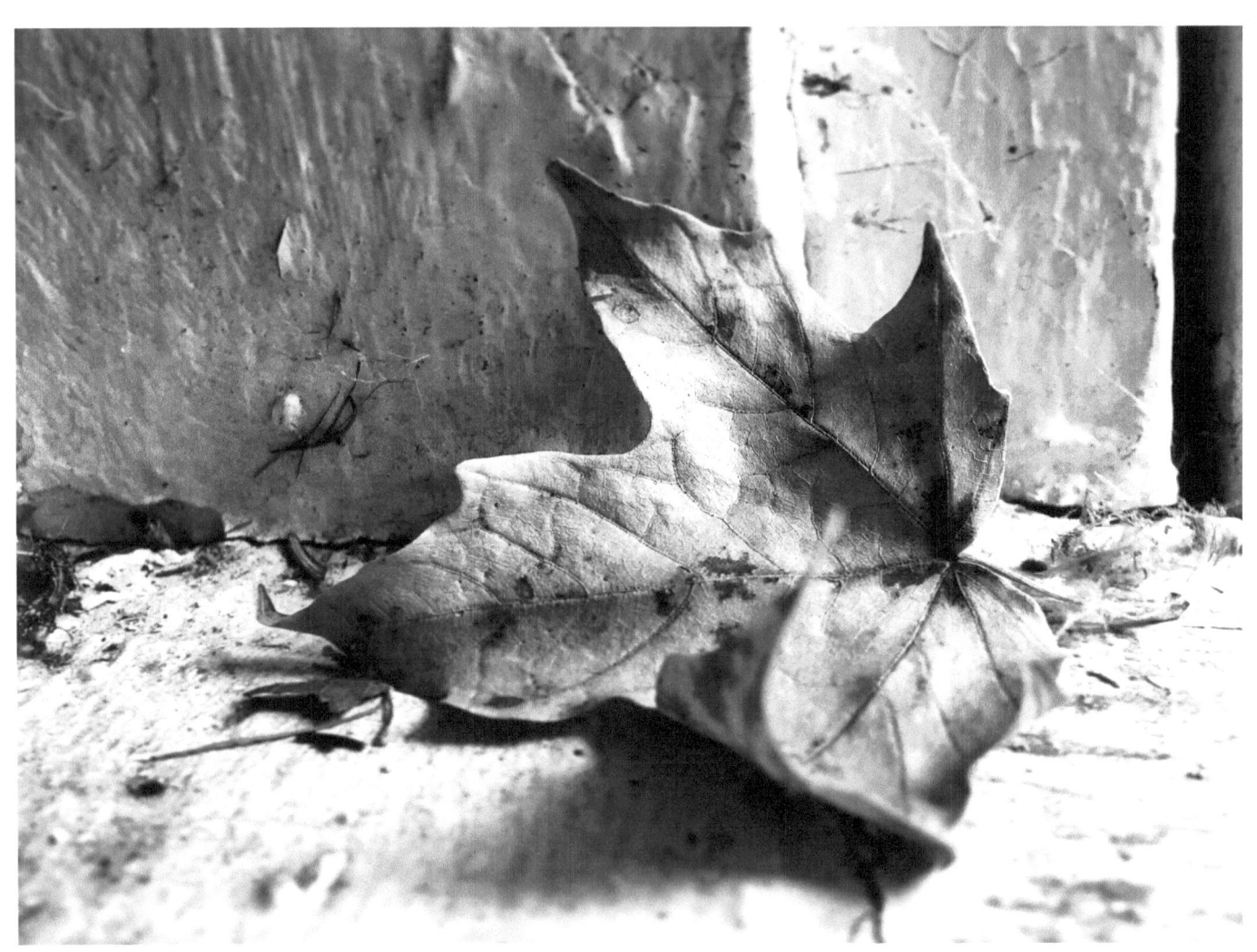

ABOUT THE ARTIST

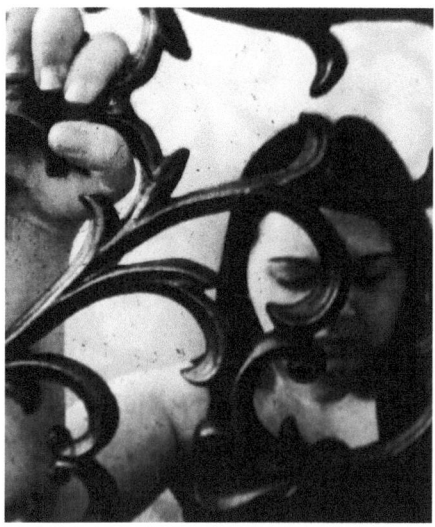

Starfleet graduate and mother of two pesky humanoid lifeforms. I dabble in writing, but my passion is photography. After my oldest broke my DSLR I decided that maybe expensive equipment wasn't for me, so I traded in my 'real equipment' for an iPhone.

I use macro lenses designed for phones for my macro work and I'm constantly learning from my mistakes.

All images are edited on the iPhone, first in Mextures, then through Instagram. Final edits are completed before printing, with only slight adjustments being made on a Mac to improve the quality of the print.

I enjoy what I do. I'm not looking for perfection, I believe flaws are a part of life and add beauty and truth to my images.

CONNECT

Instagram: @Chasingthewindphoto
Twitter: @ChasingTWphoto
Facebook: Chasing The Wind Photography

www.ingramcontent.com/pod-product-compliance
Lightning Source LLC
Chambersburg PA
CBHW051819210526
45473CB00005B/1661